A Mother's Love

by

Charlene Price

The contents of this work, including, but not limited to, the accuracy of events, people, and places depicted; opinions expressed; permission to use previously published materials included; and any advice given or actions advocated are solely the responsibility of the author, who assumes all liability for said work and indemnifies the publisher against any claims stemming from publication of the work.

All Rights Reserved
Copyright © 2024 by Charlene Price

No part of this book may be reproduced or transmitted, downloaded, distributed, reverse engineered, or stored in or introduced into any information storage and retrieval system, in any form or by any means, including photocopying and recording, whether electronic or mechanical, now known or hereinafter invented without permission in writing from the publisher.

Dorrance Publishing Co
585 Alpha Drive
Suite 103
Pittsburgh, PA 15238
Visit our website at *www.dorrancebookstore.com*

ISBN: 979-8-89127-645-1
eISBN: 979-8-89127-143-2

A Mother's Love

Where is the baby so small and sweet

With tiny hands and little feet

That stole our hearts from that first day

While sleeping in her crib she lay?

Where is the child not even two

Who smiled and giggled at peek-a-boo

Each time thereafter brought just the same

As mother and child played this game?

Where are the books that daddy read

Before he tucked her into bed

With arms around her softly bent

Was she or he the most content?

Where is the teddy she held in hand

With colored fur like golden sand

That slept with her through nap and night

When Heaven's stars brought lovely light?

Where is the child with golden hair

With eyes of blue and skin so fair

Once on beaches far away

She smiled and laughed in child's play

She dreamed of horses that she would ride

On sandy shores in ebbing tide?

Where are the fields where she did play

With wonders full of God's new day

Where treasures sweet could oft be found

As she explored things all around

The lady bug in hand so small

Trees, birds, and flowers she loved them all

Where is the tree so big and tall

Where she would climb and slowly crawl?

To peek on eggs the robins lay

Then watch for chicks another day

"Mother, mother you almost sleep

Where are your thoughts?

They must run deep."

"I was in another place

When you were young

With child's sweet face."

"Wake up, dear mother, for up I grew

And stand right here in your view

That time has passed and gone away

It's time far spent, a distant day."

"Yes, my daughter, your words are true

But tis what all we mothers do

Dream of times our hearts so treasure

That even love cannot measure

And still as time goes passing by

They oft escape on wings and fly

Oh, Mother, I know how well you miss

Those times for you that brought such bliss

More memories will come your way

As with my daughter you now play

And when you leave for Heaven's place

And we no longer see your face

In us your memory will abide

And you will walk right by our side.

9798891276451.